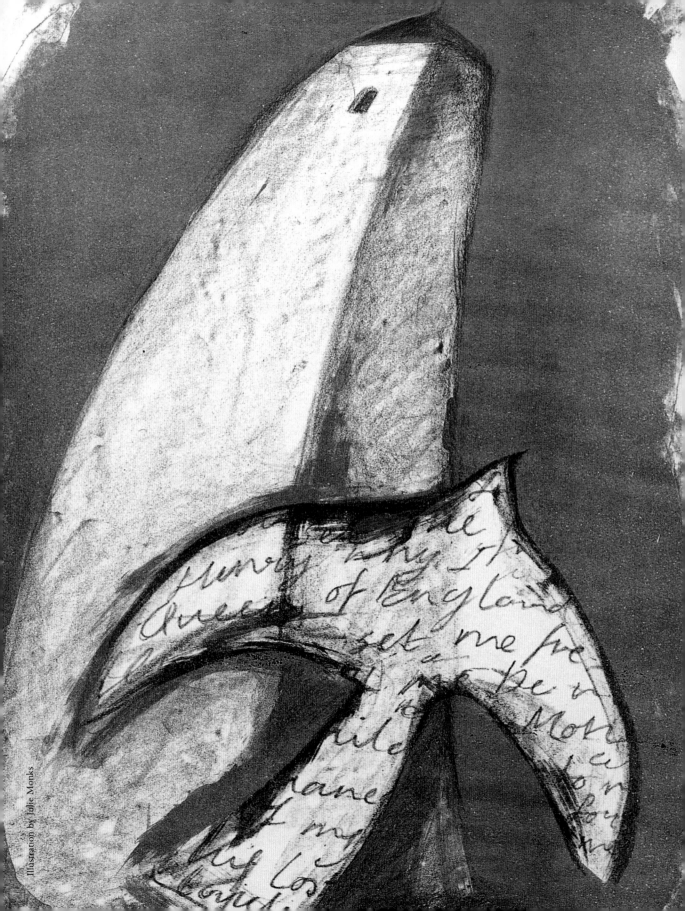

Letters of Peace

Chosen by Royal Mail from 'Young Letter-writers'

PAVILION

Book devised and designed by Newell and Sorrell

*with illustrations by students from Kingston University,
Royal College of Art, Central St Martins & Camberwell College of Art*

Letters of Peace

First published in Great Britain in 1995 by
PAVILION BOOKS LIMITED 26 Upper Ground, London SE1 9PD

This edition of the letters copyright © Pavilion Books 1995
Illustrations copyright © Newell and Sorrell 1995

The moral right of the illustrators has been asserted

Book devised and designed by Newell and Sorrell

A CIP catalogue record for this book is available from the British Library.

ISBN 1 85793 761 9

Set in Sabon, Joanna, Granjon & Stempel Garamond.
Printed in Italy by Stige

2 4 6 8 10 9 7 5 3 1

This book can be ordered direct from the publisher.
Please contact the Marketing Department. But try your bookshop first.

reading ... letter filled me
with a sense of
peace. worries seem
to take over our
lives and we can
see beyond the
passage of
time ...

Foreword by Jill Morrell

I began to really appreciate the power of letter-writing during the time that the Friends of John McCarthy were campaigning for the release of British hostages in Lebanon. We were desperate to persuade politicians here and in the Middle East to act to resolve the differences between Britain and Iran which were denying the hostages their freedom. For a long time it seemed that the letters were not helping, but I came to realise that their effect was priceless; they were one of the most effective means we had of influencing politicians, making them accountable for their actions and bringing about a peaceful resolution to the hostage problem. For this the Friends were dependent on the thousands of people all over the country who took the trouble to write those letters to politicians at home and abroad. After John McCarthy came home we were told that one of the most important factors in the hostages' release was our lobbying, in the form of these letters - letters of peace.

I know how difficult it can be to write this kind of letter, and this is why I found the entries in the Royal Mail Young Letter-writers event so impressive and why it was a privilege to be one of the judges. The standard of entries was so high that the final judging was very difficult; each author expressed their own vision of peace in an eloquent, thoughtful way which caught the imagination and stayed lodged in the mind. Each author got to the heart of the matter in hand, captured the judges' attention, and moved them. To be able to communicate in this way is a precious gift to have, especially as letter-writing can be one of the most effective ways of achieving change in our society. The time and energy that were invested in the letters in this book are apparent on every page. I found reading them inspiring, and I hope that readers of this book and young letter-writers of the future will do so.

Jill Morrell.

Illustration by Aude Van Ryn

Dear Dad

I am sorry if I am a little horror but I can't help it, but I am very sorry. It would be nice if we could stop arguing and if we could be kind to each other. If it could be peaceful it would be nice. When me and my dad argue I feel upset.

Love from

Nicholas

Nicholas Harbottle, age 7 Northampton

Illustration by Sean Carney

Dear Mr Major,

I am writing to you about sport and peace.
Through sports such as football and cricket
people can meet and make friends with
people from other countries and religions.
If people are friends they will not fight each
other. When countries do want to fight,
why don't they settle their problems on the
football or cricket field? In the old days,
kings often settled arguments with a fight
between their champion knights. The rest
of the people did not have to fight. I think
you should give lots of money for sport to
get better. This will allow people to play
instead of fighting. If we did settle things
through sport England would have a better
chance of winning.

Yours sincerely,

Neil Bustin

Neil Bustin, age 9 Five Acres C.P. School Bicester

Illustration by Sarah Markes

In The Year of our Lord, 1368
Jerusalem

Your Majesty,

I am writing to you in haste and fear of death, not only my own but also those of your loyal subjects. The Moors are all around us and have us at a disadvantage.

Following the failure of the siege of Judea, most of my army was routed and fled to the coast. Our defeat was inevitable from the start, as we attacked a force of thousands appeared, as if from nowhere, on the hills to the west of us.

They thundered towards us like the devil's hoard; severely outnumbered, we fought bravely but to no avail. We were forced to retreat to this castle in Jerusalem. I confess to foreboding about the success of this crusade and fear we may be facing failure. Perhaps my Lord would do well to consider retreating to the coast and making a final attempt to secure peace with the Moorish lords. This would serve to save the lives of many English nobles and avoid the disgrace of defeat to your Majesty.

You may consider me faithless to voice these doubts but do not, I beg you Sire, mistake them for disloyalty. Be assured that I and the loyal few I have about me will follow your orders, without question, even if it results in paying the ultimate price.

We will put our trust in God and attempt to hold fast our position until your wishes are known, despite the knowledge that you may not receive this missive in time to prevent our untimely deaths.

This letter was found in the fired ruins. Sadly the writer was dead. However I send this to the King in the hope the author does not die in vain. God willing we will have peace.

Geoffrey Lancaster
Barry Evans, age 14 Carmel School Darlington

Illustration by Peter Allsop

LOVE

friEndship

PEACE

harmony

Dear Saint Patrick

You brought religion to Ireland and made all the bad people good people and gave us a more peaceful Ireland. It is now 1994 and Ireland is full of evil people who are bombing and shooting and blaming religion for their own badness. They decide where people of different religions must live and where they can go. Dear Saint Patrick this year instead of turning the stone please turn all the bad people good people again. Guns and bombs cost lots of money, this money could help sick children's lives, it could build parks and playgrounds and community centres that everyone could enjoy. Please let them open their hearts to all the beautiful things that Ireland has, let them see how lucky we are that we have summers and winters that allow our crops to grow, we have plenty of fresh water and no starving children dying every day and helpers of all kinds to make our lives easier. So please Saint Patrick help the bad people see how lucky they are to find their goodness and bring us peace again.

Joe McAuley, age 7 Holy Cross Boys Primary Belfast

Illustration by Claire McKenna

The womb
Inside my mother PEA CE1

To my mother,

Lying here, curled up snugly inside your body, I feel peaceful. My entire surrounding area is love and warmth. I sense your emotions: happiness, sadness, joy and pain. I feel the distinctiveness between day and night. In the day, you go about your business taking extra care so as not to harm me. I hear your gentle voice only utter caring words. At night I listen to the sound of your heartbeat, gently lulling me to sleep and I know that you are there.

The comfort I feel knowing that the person who holds me within cares about me, despite knowing nothing about me, is indescribable. You protect me from harm and make me feel safe and needed. For that I am grateful. My life is in your hands and I know now that our bond has been made, that I am safe from danger. The security you feel is the security I feel, the anger and hurt you feel are all passed on to me. But I have both comfort and peace knowing that you are not alone out there. I know because I hear the voice, the deep voice of the one who cares both for you and also for me. My father.

This is my idea of peace, being cared for and looked after, feeling warm, secure and wanted and I owe all of these feelings to you. I am blessed with the knowledge that, one day in the not too distant future, I shall be able to see and touch the person who has given me this feeling of peacefulness and tranquillity throughout the beginning of my life. I know that when this time comes, I will be able to look upon this person, you, and know that she is my mum. I am eternally thankful for being able to start my life in such a peaceful way. I hope that one day, in an effort to thank you, and also my father, I will do you both proud. I want you both to feel the peace that I feel now.

Love from your child

Samantha Williams, age 14 Wentworth High School Manchester

3 March 1994

Dear World Leaders

My little sister believes that rain comes when God is very sad and cries because of all the hurt in the world. When it rains she stands at the window and, hands on hips, she shakes her head from side to side and tut tuts just like the adults she is copying when they want to show her they are unhappy at something she has done.

1994 has been a very wet year so far - it has rained a lot in Ireland; it has rained a lot in Yugoslavia; it has rained a lot in the West Bank and all over Africa from Cape Town to Angola. 1994 has been a very, very wet year, so far. And sometimes when I watch my little sister staring out at the rain beating down and her tut-tutting all the while with mock sadness and concern for God's tears, sometimes I think my mother's explanation for rainfall must be true.

When I watch the news I wonder, how can I explain to my little sister the reason why grown men would explode a mortar shell in the middle of a school playground in Bosnia? Or why a poor shoeless peasant woman in Mozambique with her baby strapped to her back had to lose her foot when she trod on a mine?

How could anyone justify these things to an innocent and inquiring mind? How could I explain the death of that poor peasant woman from the loss of blood and then the death of her baby from starvation, alone, in a field. still strapped to its mothers back with no one to hear its weakening cries?

I am old enough to know that rain is not God's tears. But I also know that God is crying somewhere. He must be crying when he sees the cruelty and madness in the world today. He has been crying for a long time now, too long. The rain has been falling since Cain fought with Abel.

The tears have been falling since pre-history, since Ghenghis-Khan stormed out of the frozen steppes to raise civilization to the ground; since Greeks fought the Turks; since the Romans fought with the known world, the Jews and the Britons.

He must have cried an ocean when babies were flung into gas chambers at Belsen and Auschwitz. And still he cried when Pol Pot made mountains from the skulls of his own people in the name of some madness in the jungles of South-East Asia.

But then I remember. I remember that every war that ever was came to an end sometime. Every conflict eventually ended. At sometime God would have decided there had been enough tears, and unseen he would work in the hearts of men and women and for a long time the world would know peace.

This I would tell my little sister. Peace will come again to Africa, to Israel, to Yugoslavia and even in the longest war in the history of the world, the 800 years of war between England and Ireland; peace will come.

The Berlin Wall is no more. Communism is gone too. Things which we thought would never change have suddenly been utterly changed. Peace will eventually come all over the world and mankind will learn to live with the dignity and nobility of which he is capable.

He will learn to live in harmony with nature like his ancestors on the plains of North America, respecting all living things and taking from the earth only as much as he needs to sustain life. When we at long last learn to view ourselves only as the caretakers of the earth, holding it in trust for future generations, then we will have learned an important truth.

Like the Indian people's knew and understood a thousand years ago when they lived in total harmony and self-sufficiency in their world we will have learned that a man cannot own a mountain or a lake or a tree. When we have realized this truth we will have become a little more civilized. Then peace will reign, and the trees of the rainforest will be preserved for the good of all, and every other animal including man himself, will sleep easier.

When this happens at some time in the future, my little sister will tell her daughter that rain comes when God cries. But the rain is caused by tears of joy falling from heaven.

Yours,

A Friend in Peace.

Grainne O'Reilly, age 14 St. Louise's Comprehensive Belfast

Illustrations by Michelle Thompson

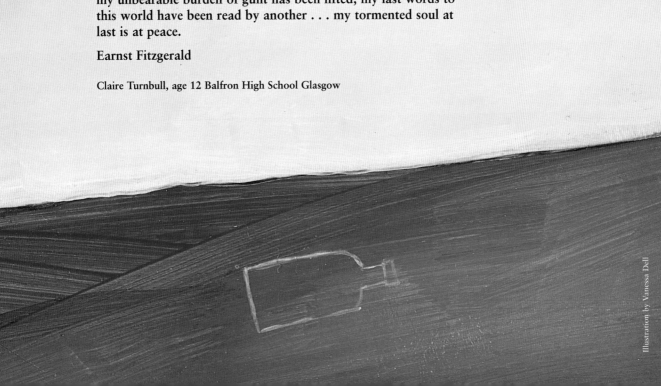

The 26th day of March
In the year of our Lord, 1658

To ye, the finder of this bottle, cast upon the waves by one who
through this act has finally found peace in his soul.
For I, Captain Earnst Fitzgerald have for fifty long and solitary
years lived a forsaken existence on an Isle, deep in the heart of
the terrible, cruel world.
Aye, fifty years ago to this very day I was thrust upon this Isle
by way of a punishment, for I did once commit a terrible crime -
I killed a fellow sailor, and a dire punishment it was indeed.
Imagine, fifty years with not another living being to talk to, save
the mindless chatter of the monkeys and the callous, heartless
mockings of the hyenas.
And I, with the terrible affliction of guilt to bear, yet no one to
unburden my remorse upon.
But, with a scrap of paper and ink salvaged from a previous life,
I was ever hoping that an opportunity would arise whereby I
could let the world know my acknowledged shame, for was ever
a decent, God-fearing man so sorely punished with no final
reprieve?
Words cannot express my ecstatic joy when a bottle was washed
up upon my shore - for it is surely a sign that God hath forgiven
me, and I may finally leave this life. . . I may die, knowing that
my unbearable burden of guilt has been lifted, my last words to
this world have been read by another . . . my tormented soul at
last is at peace.

Earnst Fitzgerald

Claire Turnbull, age 12 Balfron High School Glasgow

Sunny Cottage Brookend POR 1GE

Dear Bears,
If you remember a little while ago I broke into your cottage. I am very sorry for eating your porridge, breaking baby bear's chair and sleeping in your bed. I would like to make my peace with you. I told my mother what I had done. She told me to write this letter to you. I hope you accept my apology. I will not do it again.
Yours sincerely,

Goldilocks

Martina Gallogly, age 8 St Joseph's Primary School Ederney

Illustration by Ed Taylor

Verona, 1594

Dear Lady Montague,

After much careful thought and deliberation I have come to the conclusion that
I must be the one to make the effort to reach across the barriers of this feud that
separates our two families. This bitter hatred that scars fair Verona and poisons
the minds of those living inside her walls shall continue to cause much
suffering and hate unless something is done to free us from this ancient grudge.
Therefore, I feel it is my obligation to bring about a means of communication

which would undoubtedly result in a much less hostile
atmosphere. Good Lady I beseech you, hear what I have to
say now and do not discard this letter, for it is this, and
only this, that will convey my sincerest wishes. Therefore,
let me reflect upon the untimely death of Mercutio and
then of my dearest cousin Tybalt, both of whom were
slain through a rage of mistempered hate. This would be
woe enough if it had ended there, but upon this darkened
fate Romeo has been taken from us, to a place far worse
than death itself. My foolish tears are not wept for Tybalt
but for the villain who killed him, Madam, when this
horrific deed was done, I was three hours his wife. Now
hear me with patience whilst I declare my undying love
for your son Romeo. How my heart yearns for his name and yet I know we shall
never meet again - for fate has led us both down a path of misguided sorrow.
I fear there will be no end to our suffering unless an end can be brought to this
deadly quarrel and in so doing, reversing the Prince's judgement and so
relinquishing the invisible boundaries that keep Romeo and I apart. Dear Lady,
I must now conclude for night draws in. I sincerely hope that you will deem
my words of peace worthy of your consideration.

Yours in anticipation,

Juliet Capulet

Julia Moffat, age 13 Soham Village College Soham Ely

Illustration by Kes James

Dear Lord of Peace,

Last night there was a terrifying storm.
The wind rattled my bedroom window and
the rain lashed down.
I could not sleep, I watched the lightning as
it lit up my room.
In the morning came sunrise.
The rain had made the grass sparkle like a
million diamonds and the first noise I heard
was the singing of the birds.
If you can make peace, surely anyone can.

From Rebecca

Rebecca Marriott, age 7 Crockerton Primary School Warminster

To the man with a clipboard,

We have seen a lot of you this week - that must mean the diggers are coming. Yesterday I saw a sign next to the wood saying 'chemical factory being built'! The Squirrelshire

Council had a meeting last night and decided that someone should write to you. I was chosen. All I want to say is that you will spoil the beautiful, peaceful wood we live in where the birds sing and play with other animals all under the sunshine coming through the trees and shining on to the beautiful coloured plants.

BUT if you build the chemical factory next to our wood, it will spoil it. The air will be filled with noise and pollution. Our animals breath the air in and if you build the factory it will probably kill our animals. So your chemical factory will spoil our lives and the environment. The smoke will cover where the sun shines through and the wood will be darkness. You don't have to build on woods and countryside - you can build on wasteland. So please, please leave us in peace, and other countrysides as well. Thank you from Squirrelshire Council Leader

Simon Squirrel

Graham Sykes, age 7 Hilton Primary School Derby

Illustration by Leonie Lord

Dear Virginia Bottomley,

My granny has been waiting for two years now for her operation. Most of the time she is in a lot of pain. The hospital where she was to have her operation you have now closed so now she has got to go on another waiting list in another hospital so it will take even longer now.

Can you change your silly rules and free my granny from pain and let her live a peaceful, happy life? Please re-open the hospital near my home.

Yours sincerely,

Siobhan Sippy

Siobhan Sippy, age 8 St Anselms School Harrow-on-the-Hill

Illustration by Alyson Waller

'The Kennel' Bishopton Road Stockton
Cleveland

Dear Blackie,

Isn't it time we call a truce, aim at a reconciliation, bury the hatchet, hold out the olive branch, heal the breach, restore harmony, or just simply

... Make Peace?

We've waged war now for about eight years! I remember when I first set eyes on you shortly after I moved in here with the Straughan family. You were sitting on my new garden fence. Not for long! You knew then that you no longer had feline right of way over my garden. Then there was that hot July day when the Straughans were sitting on the front lawn eating strawberries and I was having forty winks after licking clean a big juicy marrow bone. I just happened to raise one eyelid and what did I see? YOU - walking coolly up my drive in that haughty, swaggering way that you have! I couldn't believe my eyes. Well, then the fun started! I hurtled to my feet and set off over the strawberries, over the dishes and over the Straughans. The victory that day was yours - although perhaps you did not know it. You see, I was in disgrace for ruining the

'strawberries-on-the-lawn' session. I was sent to my kennel early with the sounds of 'bad dog' and 'that dog will have to go' ringing in my ears. I kept my head down well between my paws that night, I can tell you.

Just last week, when you were chasing that mouse near the greenhouse, there was more trouble. I don't like mice BUT if there are mice in my garden, then I'm the one who is going to do the chasing - thank you! No one was the victor that time. You sat in the plum tree hissing and spitting as usual. I sat underneath yowling with frustration that I couldn't get at you - the poor mouse lay down and died of heart failure (inspite of Philip's attempts to revive it!). Of course, there have been many more skirmishes between us - but don't you think we're both getting a bit old for all this? I've got this thing the vet calls arthritis in the old front legs and I notice that you don't scale those trees as fast as you used to!

What about making the gardens of Bishopton Road a more peaceful place? Should we shake paws, settle our difference, wave the white flag ... LIVE IN PEACE? Give it some thought, will you?

From your old adversary,
Lucy the Labrador

WINNER Philip Straughan, age 10 Cleveland

Illustration by Gill Button

Dear Grandad and gerbils

I hope you like it up in heaven

This is your chance to

have a proper sleep

and have peace.

Scott Elliott, age 7 St Gregory's R.C. Primary School Cheltenham

Love from Scot

Tower of London

19th day of May, Year of Our Lord, 1536

Sire,

I, Anne, come from Traitor's Gate to the Tower and await my execution with the knowledge I am innocent of treason and appeal to you for peace between us. Our two-year-old daughter Elizabeth will be motherless and I hope in time I shall give you a much longed for son. The accusations made against me of having paramours are wickedly untrue.

Perhaps I am no beauty but my wit and personality has always pleased you, Henry, and fables of my mark of the devil by having six fingers are perhaps true as I once bewitched you from Catherine of Aragon.

An axe from France has been ordered to be brought for my execution - a common axe is not good enough for me - the Queen of England and mother of your child. I beg of you Henry make peace with my brother and myself. What good is there in this quarrel between us?

Let me be a good and faithful Queen of England.

My words I know are in vain as the hour of my death approaches.

I wonder who will follow in my footsteps as Queen? Will it be the sickly Jane Seymour? And then, I pause and wonder who will be the last wife of the noble King Henry VIII.

Anne Boleyn

Queen of England

Jane Moffat, age 10 Gretna Primary Gretna

46

19th day of May, 1536

SIRE

I, Anne, come from

T..tor's Gate to

Tower and

..cutio..

Dear Mr Beethoven

I am sitting in my bedroom listening to a recording of your sixth symphony. It is a sunny spring day and I live in the centre of London. It is noisy, far noisier than cities were in your day, and quite smelly.

When I close my eyes whilst listening to this music, I imagine that I am far away from the bustling city. It calms me down and I imagine that I am running through green fields feeling a breeze blowing in my face. I sit under a tree and listen to the birds singing gently, and even see a fox cub peeking through the bushes. I smell freshly cut grass and sweet scented flowers. Children play and dance around me, and even the rain makes us happy.

I know that as you grew older and more sick you were a sad, frustrated man and not all your music is happy. I love all your music but this symphony is like sunshine in the spring. I wish I could play it on a giant loudspeaker all over the world to help calm people who are cruel and wicked to each other, both grown-ups and children. Thank you, Mr Beethoven. If I could compose one little piece of music as beautiful as this I would feel that I had given something good to the world.

Yours sincerely,
Charles Siem

Charles Siem, age 8 St Paul's Preparatory School London

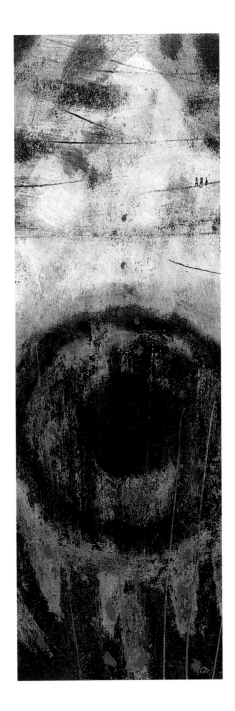

27 Highrising, Finchampsted 21/3/94

Dear Peter,

Greetings! I have just returned from my expedition to Nanga Parbat with the team. I enclose the photos I promised you. What struck me most about the mountains was their overpowering calm. This was only my second eight-thousander and I loved every minute of it. The mountain rises above all other peaks, its majestic beauty offering a challege to any that pass it.

On the ascent I found it very tough going. We went up the Diamir face. The size of it is overwhelming. When we reached 5,000 metres air was beginning to get very thin. Movement of any description was difficult and required much effort. On the sixth day I rose early. As I clambered out of my tent I stopped and listened. I could hear nothing. However, hearing nothing wasn't like being on your own in the middle of a graveyard at night. It was a peaceful nothing. I felt, for the first time on the expedition, at peace with my surroundings. It was just me and the mountain.

We conquered the peak in the end,which was very pleasing. Our descent was fairly straightforward and took minimal time. When I returned, I learned about the tragic death of those climbers on Ben Nevis. I suppose it brought home to me the fact that underneath the peace and serenity, mountains will always hold that deadly power. Now I must go, but I wish you every success in your expedition to K2.

Let me know how you get on!

Until then, Your good friend,

James

James Woolrich, age 12 Wokingham Berkshire

Illustration by Sarah Markes

To a little girl in Sarajevo,

I look at your country, and I see fighting. I hear
guns firing and people screaming. Then I look at
my country and I see children playing. I hear birds
singing and people laughing.
But what can I do?
If I could I would send you my teddy bear to
cuddle when you are sad.
I would send you my doctor to make you well
again if you get injured.
If I could I would send you a sunny day with
children playing happily together and you could
join in and smile again.
I would send you the quiet like a cold winter
morning and I would send you my hand to hold
when the guns are shooting all around.
But really I can't send you any of these, so instead
I will send you this thought of peace, that one day
will happen - I promise.

From Adele
From England

WINNER Adele Rebecca Hardy, age 7 Horsley Woodhouse Primary School Ilkeston

Illustrations by Tiphanie Beeke

Readers Digest Berkeley Square House London W1

Dear Sir/Madam

I write to you to request that you publish the follow poem which I have written about peace. Everyone in the world has their own idealistic opinion of peace. In my poem I have tried to convey as many different ideas of peace imaginable. With all the disharmony, conflict and troubles in today's society, I hope that this poem will strike a note of peace with everyone who reads it. I dedicate my creation especially to the people of the former Yugoslavia, all the warring nations of the world, the sick, the lonely, the depressed and whoever strives for peace on earth.

Peace could be . . .

Peace could be a sunny spell
On a tumultuous rainy day.
Or it could be the eye of the storm
Before the hurricane has its way.

Peace could be the end of conflict
Among the warring factions of the world.
And hence the signatures of their leaders
On a treaty or declaration unfurled.

Peace could be a desert island,
No civilization for miles around.
Sitting in our solitude,
No distractions, disturbances or sounds.

Peace could be a dear one,
Lying lifeless in their grave.
You know now how much more peaceful
they are,
Yet remember all the love they gave.

Peace could be the feeling of tranquility
At the holy grotto in Lourdes.
That spiritual knowledge of healing,
People hoping that they will be cured.

Peace could be heaven
After life's passed you by.
No troubles or worries
With God when you die.

Peace could be a walk through the woods
On a fresh spring day.
Where one sees the daffodils, tulips
and snowdrops,
United in a colourful floral display.

Peace could be an image
Like the tranquil, silent dove;
Symbolic to many nations,
Showing serenity and love.

Everyone has different ideas of peace,
But the most important thing to see,
Is that peace comes from the heart,
And is only what you want it to be.

I thank you for reading my poem and I hope you see fit to publish it. It is very important to me that I get this message across to many people in the world, including those engaged in battle. Hopefully, after reading this, it will encourage them to give up the fighting and lay down their arms once and for all.

Yours faithfully,

Olivia Gilchrist

Olivia Gilchrist, age 14 Assumption Grammar Ballynahinch Co. Down

Dear Laura,

Where I live it is peaceful. I'll try to describe it for you.
In the evening I can hear the gentle breezes and the sunsets
are beautiful. On a peaceful, calm day in summer I can sit
on a beach and watch the puffins fly freely in the sky. I can
paddle in little ponds and burns, watching the water going
off towards the horizon.

I have friendly neighbours up in Shetland - like if you are
hurt they will come and help you to your home. No one in
Shetland is left on their own to die because everyone knows
each other and helps each other.

There is lovely scenery up in Shetland like beautiful hills
and tremendous cliffs, cool, clear streams and spectacular
green meadows full of green grass. When you wake up you
can hear the lambs bleating to their mums.

In Shetland you can buy great food like fresh seafood and
good baked bread.

On a sunny summer's day you can take your rucksack and
go to climb a hill to see the gorgeous scenery. But in war,
areas like Bosnia, Northern Ireland and Palestine, they don't
get peace like I do up in Shetland.

In winter you can go outside and play in the snow with
your sledges. Some days I go by myself and look at the old
castles.
I wish you could come for your holidays.
Love from

Donna

Donna Robertson, age 7 Olnafirth Primary School Voes Shetland

Illustration by Marnie Yuen

Western Front 25/12/1914

Dear Mum and Dad

Are you well? I am but it is very
muddy and rat infested in the
trenches. It is bitterly cold. You'll
never guess what happened

yesterday. The Germans started singing songs and shouting
'come over here'. One of our 'nuts' climbed out and waltzed
towards the German fence and was met about halfway by a
German soldier. They shook hands and became quite friendly.
Today we all played football even though we were tired. The
score was 3-2 to the Germans. We showed photographs of our
families and swapped cigars and cigarettes. It is so quiet and
peaceful considering there is no noise of gunshots and shells.
Germans are not that bad after all. I wish it was always like this.
From your loving son,

Alexander

Alexandra Mewha, age 8 Greenway School Berkhamsted

Dear Mr Major,

A little boy wanders
through war torn streets
looking for his mother.
Every now and then he
crouches in fear as another
bomb explodes. He looks
up and sees a dove in the
blue sky. The boy cries out
for help to the world to
bring peace to his Bosnia.
Yours sincerely,

Nicola Rollinson

Nicola Rollinson, age 7 Coteswood House School Nottingham

Illustration by Sarah Markes

This is an angry letter from a thirteen-year-old girl to her soldier father who is on duty in Northern Ireland.

19/02/94

Dad

I don't suppose you remember that you now have a TEENAGE daughter, but once upon a time you used to live with me in a tiny, boring little flat in a boring little town with no nice war for you to play in and a wife and a son. WELL?? Do you ever think about your ten year old son? Yeah! That's strange because he's eleven now. He's looking for a secondary school actually. We're not children.

You send all our money but don't think we need you or anything like that because Mum could work, she could have a proper job.

Don't tell me it will all be O.K. in a few months and we'll all live happily ever after in a big country house because it won't work anymore. You KNOW you'll probably die in conflict. I'm sorry to be so blunt but it's time you faced up to the truth. They're going to get you!

No, actually, I'm not sorry, Dad. Of all the jobs you could take, you signed up to join a group where killing is sanctioned. How many families will you devastate, will you ever stop to think about that before you pull the trigger? Some woman will be widowed, some child fatherless. Just like we might lose you some day.

It's not your quarrel, Dad, you don't hate these people, will you kill someone just because you're told to?

It's pathetic, the way Jamie looks up to you like some god and runs around the house pretending to shoot me but is afraid of the dark and being left in the house alone. You should talk to him about what it's really like in a war.

On the other hand, I can feel ashamed to say what your profession is. When people ask me what you do, I call you a civil servant, because you work for the Government really, don't you?

What's the point in calling us a family if we're never together. Mum tells me that I've got to be brave too, but she knew you were a soldier when she married you. I didn't choose to be a soldier's daughter, did I? Do you ever think about us Dad? How often? Am I in your mind when you wake up and when you go to sleep? Do you dream about me? It's about your priorities, isn't it? Who's the important ones, us or

the army? Or are you doing it for England? Well I don't want to give you up for England, I want you to be here for us.

You might be in the army to appease your conscience but I know you could do an equally worthy job for charity or something and not be blown up. Can you answer me this: in what way does your job promote peace for anyone?

Caroline

20/02/94

Dear Daddy

If you want to know why I was crying on the phone yesterday, it was because of what I'd already written in this letter.

I am sorry, very sorry, not because I've changed my mind but because of the hurtful things I've written. However, I am sending you the whole, uncensored letter so you know how worried I feel sometimes, when I miss you.

Don't bother being angry at me, I've heard it all before. Mum saw the letter and just exploded, saying how ungrateful and vindictive I was etc. She doesn't know I've sent it, I secretly made a second print before she burnt the other one and destroyed the file on the hard disk.

No, I think you ought to understand some of the bad feelings I have, because pretending nothing's ever wrong is treating you like a child when you're a man, and very brave, just brave about the wrong things.

The fact that you have read this far, despite all the terrible things I've said, shows you care. Thanks.

I've realized now that your life is yours to do what you want with. Although I love you and don't want to lose you, I know that you don't belong to me and I have no right to influence your decision.

I hope you understand that I wouldn't have written that awful letter yesterday if I didn't love you. As you do not live in a peaceful atmosphere it's extra important that I do not spoil our relationship by antagonizing you.
Love from

Caroline

Jenny Pagdin, age 14 Wycombe High School
Marlow Hill High Wycombe

Dear Mosquito,

As the summer is coming soon, I decided to write you
a letter so we are both prepared for the troubles. In the
past summers we had some trouble during many, many
sleepless nights. I have been listening to the buzzing
noises made by you and your brothers. It sounded like
fifty-five World War 2 fighter aircraft circling around my
head. I am sorry I killed one of your brothers by my air
defence systems. If you want to avoid more bloodshed,
you better listen to this. I am offering you peace, if you
obey the following rules:

1 I will leave a cup of blood by the front door for you
2 You are not allowed to sting any people from my family
3 That applies to your brothers too
4 You are only allowed to drink blood from the cup one
   at a time
5 If you obey the rules peace will start in the summer

Buzz, buzz, buzz.

Yours stingerely,

Buzzhew
(Matthew Jacobs zzzz)

Matthew Jacobs, age 7 Garden Suburb Junior School London

Illustration by Jane Webster

To my Mum,

I don't like fighting.
I hate blood.
I want peace.

Rejwan Ahmed, age 4 Tiverton School Birmingham

Rejwan

My dear English friends

What really peace means, nobody can understand until you lose that peace. In Europe there was a country which was called Yugoslavia. This country had six republics and one of them was my Bosnia.

In Bosnia three different nations used to live together. These nations were Muslims, Serbs and Croats. We thought that our country was the most beautiful country in the world and that Bosnian people were the happiest people on the world. Bosnian people

were happy and they often used to have parties where all different nations used to be together. Lots of people had mixed marriages. There were so many mixed marriages that most of us didn't know if they were Muslims, Croats or Serbs simply that we were all Bosnian. I am a child from a mixed marriage.

I don't know why and neither do my parents, but two years ago the peace went away from our small country and happiness disappeared. The people were happy no more, there were no smiles on their faces and they were not as beautiful as before. Somebody taught them that they were different. Now people hate each other and they don't know why. They hate each other simply because somebody is telling them that they are not the same and that they have to be enemies. They are the people who yesterday lived peacefully together and are now on different sides, now they are killing each other and seeing their freedom in the disappearance of the other nations.

One nice spring day we had to leave our house, our town, our country. Our parents wanted to save our lives, our dad didn't want to be a soldier and kill somebody and that's why we had to go. Friends of my dad and mum took our house but people who we had never seen before helped us. Here we started a new life and we met new friends. We miss our house, our friends and our Bosnia. Very often I am sad when I see old people walking with their grandchildren because I don't know if my grandparents are still alive and if I will ever see them again. Friends from my street now live in different parts of the world: in Sweden, France, Croatia, Serbia and Bosnia. I am most worried for the ones who stayed in Bosnia. On the news I heard that people in my town died from hunger.

It's not easy, we lost everything. I only have a few pictures from my childhood but my mum says that we are all together, alive and healthy, that we didn't watch our friends dying or see our town disappearing. In England it's nice for us but we are unhappy because we are born Bosnian where our family and friends are suffering and going through hell.

If you want to keep peace, if you want to be happy you must know that all people have a soul and that you should not do to anybody else what you don't want somebody else to do to you. Do not divide people on white, black or yellow. If you help others, one day when you need, you can be sure that somebody will help you. Let all nationalities live together in harmony in Great Britain. Keep your peace because peace is the richest thing in the world. Be certain, I can tell you that because I know it. I hope that one day peace will come back to Bosnia and that I will be able to visit my friends the Muslims, Serbs and Croats, because they are all still my friends and I still love them the same as I used to.

Sanja Soldat

Sanja had been in England for eighteen months when she wrote this letter and did not speak any English when she arrived. English is not spoken at home.

WINNER Sanja Soldat, age 9
Haydon Abbey County Combined School Aylesbury

Illustrations by Xavier Pick

Dear Guru Gobind Singh

I am writing this letter to let you know about the wars going on around this world. Please come down to Earth from heaven and make the world peaceful and a better place to live in. Please come and stop the wars, crime, killing and everything that makes the world unhappy.

Specially of all stop the war in Bosnia and former Yugoslavia. I hear about it on the news every day and it makes me sad.

Please, please stop the wars so everyone will be happy. I shall be very, very grateful of you. Thanks.

Love from, Simranjit

Simranjit Singh Bhinder, age 10
Norwood Green Junior School Southall

Illustration by Rokeya Khanom

To the president of Iraq,
I would like a piece of cherry cake

A piece of sky
A piece of apple pie
A piece of seaside rock
A piece of Cadbury's choc

But all I really want is a peaceful world

From Joe

Joseph Buckingham age 7 Beckley School Church Lane Oxford

Illustration by Eugenie Biddle

Dear Brazil,

Please stop cutting down your rainforests. They are home to lots
of different plants, animals, birds and people. If you carry on
cutting down trees lots of animals and birds would become
extinct. Your rainforests are loved by the many people who live in
them. They do no harm, but you harm them. They just want to
live peacefully, but you destroy their homes. Please stop! Think
about the animals. Many animals live in the rainforests. Without
the rainforests they could become extinct. Soon the world would
have no more animals except pets. How would you like that?
It would be horrid. Think of all the different birds: toucans,
parrots and lots more. You would be destroying their lives.
How would you like it if you were a toucan and humans were
destroying your life? I know I'd hate it. Please stop!
What about plants? There are rare species of plants in your
rainforest. Soon they will die.
You will die because there will be no oxygen left because trees
breathe carbon dioxide and breathe out oxygen. Please, please
stop! Surely you don't want to die.
Yours faithfully,

Amy Beaumont

Amy Beaumont, age 7 Budbrooke Combined School Hampton Magna

Illustrations by Aude von Ryn

Dear Oliver Cromwell,

I'm bored of this war, aren't you? Let's get back to the old days, shall we? I'm surprisingly short of infantry and some of your men look sick. If you lend me money if I desperately need it, I'll discuss it with you. And, in case you haven't realized, we are becoming more and more unpopular with our men. Even now, people are probably plotting against us! Also France and Holland are looking nasty! Ireland is really whacking you and the East is giving me problems. There is also reports of a plague spreading across England. And we really must keep on with our foreign conquests. We've nearly captured New England and Australia! We've got to stop this war. I hope you agree with me. With kind regards,

Charles I

Matthew Houston, age 8 Portishead C. P. School Bristol

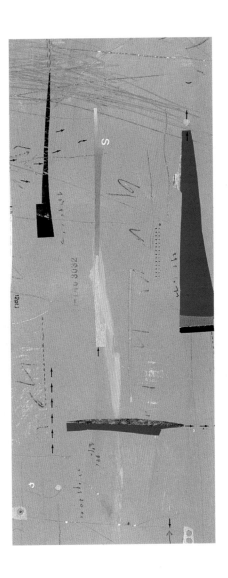

Illustration by Sara Fanelli

Dear Eve,

I can see you there, standing unashamedly naked. Beauty and peace surround you and yet you are about to give it all away to fulfill a typically human trait, curiosity. I beg of you, do not bite the tempting flesh until you have read and contemplated my words.

I write this now, my head full of clichés about the world and surroundings: the bubbling stream, quietly meandering through the lush green landscape; break the flesh, the stream darkens, bubbling chemically, the lush landscape dries to a withered mass. Fluffy, billowing clouds gently roll in the luminescent sky; break the flesh, the sky is filled with glinting skyscrapers and stone chimneys, spewing mottled smoke. The sky greys, the clouds are never ending.

The blazing sun gently warms the earth, coaxing the bright flowers to spread their delicate arms; break the flesh, the sun blazes violently, earth's core a mass of seething, turbulent lava. Poles melt, water rushes unceasing, destroying all in its path.

Creed, colour, race is incomprehensible, black stands hand in hand with white; break the flesh, man sees only in black and white, bitterness, slaughter, ignorance. A child lies peacefully sleeping in the arms of his adoring mother; break the flesh, the mother thins, her once sparkling eyes dull to deep, dark pools of misery. The child is left helpless, solitary, tears in his darkened eyes.

Land of plenty, honey and milk freely flow, the air encaptures the sounds of laughter, peace and contentment; break the flesh, the land is bare and barren, the stale air encaptures nothing but the stench of rotting corpses and the piteous moans of ghost-like humans, as they rake the arid ground with bleeding fingers in desperate search of nourishment.

Countries have no barriers, people no leaders, weapons unheard of; break the flesh, metal glints, blood flows freely, harmony is obliterated, the earth is churned. So please, Eve, think on these things before you eat. Lay the apple down and look around. What more could you want or need. Open your eyes and realize that the world's future depends on you, one bite and all will be lost; the original innocence, the original tranquility, the peace that was meant to be.

Ellen Miller

Ellen Miller, age 13 St Leonard's School St Andrews

Illustration by Lisa Wright

Dear All Human Beings,

As I look at you all, I see you inventing lots of different things. I have seen everything. I have seen the pyramids built, Christ crucified, the Viking raids, the Mary Rose sink and the first spaceship zoom up into the sky towards me. Apart from your being very intelligent, you are also very foolish. You are always fighting. From battles at castles, the battle at Waterloo to now - and you are still fighting. Why? Do you not know of peace? There is war in what used to be Yugoslavia, you are fighting in Ireland. There was the Gulf War, the Falklands War - and all because of a small argument. There is no need to fight. Why can't you just be friends for once? You are all jealous of each other. If someone has something you want, you just take it - or fight for it. You are always thinking of yourselves, of what you want. You are so selfish. Most people think that peace is a calm summer's day with a lovely blue sea, with fluffy white clouds floating across the sky. May be you think of peace as a beautiful sunset over the sea with curving, rippling waves. People who have been at war with others know what peace is. Peace is love, freedom, friendship and having a home to live in. People with kind, cheery, loving faces waiting to welcome you. Peace is lovely. Nice and quiet and tranquil. When peace is around, there is a happy feeling for everyone. The poorest to the richest person. A person with lots of friends to a person with no friends at all. Where I live peace reigns the land and everyone is happy. The only time when we are not happy is when someone disturbs our peaceful world. Have you ever noticed the contrast between your land and mine? It is strange. One minute you are walking along and the next minute there is war all around you. It is like . . . you are crossing a sort of fence. In one part of land one moment and in another part the next. It would be wonderful if we could remove the 'division line' and differences between our lands.

Yours faithfully,
The Man in the Moon

PS. I write on behalf of myself and all creatures on the Moon.

Claire Hennell, age 10
Martin Roe Junior School Nottingham

Illustration by José Touceda

Dear Debbie,

How are you? I'm sorry I haven't written for ages but I have been quite busy. Still, that's no excuse for not even taking a moment to put pen to paper. I hope you enjoyed your weekend in London! I had a fabulous holiday, although we didn't really do anything out of the ordinary. Having said that, I came across something that really intrigued me and I would like to tell you about it.

Knowing what an avid stamp collector I am, you won't be surprised to learn that whilst on holiday I went to a stamp collectors' fayre. There I found a Victorian stamp which I have always wanted for my collection. It was attached to an envelope and inside the envelope I found an old letter. Curious about its contents, I decided to read it. I know you will find this strange, but reading the letter filled me with a sense of peace. This was nothing more than a simple letter between friends. It was similar to the kind of letters we send each other. The writer, a girl called Annie, must have been about the same age as us, and she told her friend, Cecilia of her excitement at the prospect of going on holiday. She lovingly described her pet dog, and told of her worries about a school examination.

You may wonder why this gave me inner peace. The answer is that it made me realize that people in the past were really no different from us. They worried about the same kinds of things as we do now: unemployment, war and famine - and they feel happy about the same things as us: good report cards and doing well at school and sport. Somehow, realizing this made me at peace with my own life. Often, our worries seem to take over our lives and we cannot see beyond them. They seem to be so serious and important, but really we should not worry so much. The passage of time corrects everything.

Annie will no longer be alive today and so I think, what was the point of worrying? Life is too short to worry. This pacifies me to a great extent. But anyway, enough of this philosophical talk. I hope you understand what I'm trying to say!

How are Craig and Suzi Fat Cat? I hope Suzi hasn't been filling herself with too much raspberry ripple ice-cream again!

Well, I think that's all. I hope to see you soon.

Lots of love,
Your friend forever!
Elizabeth

PS. Annie's old letter also made me realize what great things letters are, since they can last for such a long time and can even bring happiness and peace to someone hundreds of years later. Therefore I promise I will write more regularly in future!

WINNER Elizabeth Sutton, age 12 Ayrshire

Dear BBC,

Whenever I switch on the television there is always war, violence and cruelty. Why doesn't the television ever influence the world to have peace and hope? All adults' programmes are mostly about killing, war and arguments. Nowadays even a simple children's cartoon of Tom and Jerry is all fighting and violence. The news shows war, death and destruction. I accept that, but

surely there's some good news in the world that can cheer us up and put a smile on our faces.

How I long to see peace in the world. The BBC comes into all our homes so please show us happiness, faith and hope instead of sorrow.

Why can't you follow nature's example. After the dead, bleak winters tiny buds appear on the trees and blossom. When spring flowers peep up through the earth to make the world full of beautiful colours, the world is filled with hope.

Children copy what they see on television so could you please put more positive, exciting, peaceful ideas into our heads.

Thank you for your help.

Yours sincerely,

Baruch Baigel

Baruch Baigel, age 10 Rosh Pinah Junior School Edgware

Illustration by Gary Blight

To: 17 Highway to Heaven Cloud Road Angelton
From: 16 Spook Street Ghost Town Spiriton

Dear God,

I am writing to complain about the state of the world. I float around all day, watching what is going on in the world. The killings in Bosnia, the starvation in Ethiopia and Zambia. Little children dying and others with just days to live. I would like to know what you are going to do about it. Are you still in charge or have you left us to our own devices?

Peace is what the world needs, no more fighting, no more bloodshed. My idea of peace is no fighting, no racism, no prejudice, and most of all no war. Why do you allow people to feel that they can just take over other countries? Why do people feel that other races and religions are inferior to theirs? This is wrong - everybody is the same, we all have flesh and blood and we all have feelings. Just because people have different views and ideas doesn't mean that we're not the same inside.

I am not saying that everyone should be friends and get on well with each other, but if you don't like someone then stay away from them. That is the only way to stop fighting and get some worthwhile activities going, like saving the trees, supporting the World Wildlife Federation. There are better things to do than argue and fight.

When are you going to do something about it? Now that I have given you something to think about, I hope that you will do something about the state of the world.

Yours sincerely,

J. Jones

Jadie Jones, age 15 St Ilan School Caerphilly Mid Glamorgan

Dear Mr Major

We could make places in England better. I think
we should leave the M25 alone. Why do we need
it bigger? Things like that do not make England
peaceful. It is not fair on the animals because
people are destroying their homes. The M25 is
big enough already. We should not destroy the
countryside. We would not like it if the animals
came to destroy our homes, so why do we
destroy theirs? We should make peace with
everyone. Animals know how to make peace.
Peace is when we don't fight, so can't we be like
that? Try to save the animals because now you see
them - soon you won't.

From Dane

Dane Vallejo, age 7 St Cuthbert's R.C. Primary School Egham

Illustration by Austin Cowdall

To The Archbishop of Canterbury, Dr George Carey

Your Eminence,

I am sure you will agree that the Church is the embodiment of all that is good, honest and true in the world today, and when these virtues are in danger of becoming tarnished by 'in-fighting' it is time to plead for peace.

Nowhere can man feel more at peace with himself than in the secluded cloisters of a cathedral, and nowhere can he feel more at one with his fellow man than in the stillness of the sanctuary. Yet this peace is threatened by the controversy surrounding the ordination of women priests.

If the Church fights within itself, then there is little it can tell a wayward world; if it indulges in public disagreement it becomes fettered and bound in its aim to preach a gospel of harmony and concord. How can we see goodness in intolerance, or stability in uncertainty? Where is the 'peace which passeth all understanding' in a Church divided, or 'kind affection' in the heated, vitriolic argument of the pro and anti protagonists.

After decades of campaigning, women have finally won their place at the altar alongside men, and whether we agree or disagree with their ordination, we must surely agree that any continued disharmony can only further damage the Church's cause in a world which needs little excuse to criticize or condemn.

These disagreements must be put to one side, these arguments must come to an end and peace must reign for the sake of the unity and growth of the Church. As dawn follows after the long night, let peace follow after discord; as strength comes after weakness and song after sadness, let us see unity evolve from the disagreements of these past years.

Petty squabbles and imagined slights have no place in a Church which is seeking to lead by example. Let us make sure that our Church's example is one of love and peace, now and in years to come.

Yours pleadingly,

William Wesley

Dewi Thomas, age 14 Cefn Saeson Comprehensive School West Glamorgan

Illustration by Maya Rowson

Dear Mum

I am writing to you to ask you if you could make my sister be quiet for a few seconds. Now I see why her nickname is **Foghorn Fanny,** with her loud music. I don't mind you teaching her drama, but could you make her a miming expert - you know, the stuff without words. And then you wonder why there are no birds in the garden. But the worst thing is at night when you put her to bed, you put me to bed too.

Love from Robbie

Robbie Jarvis, age 7 Rustington C.P. School Rustington

Illustrations by Jane Webster

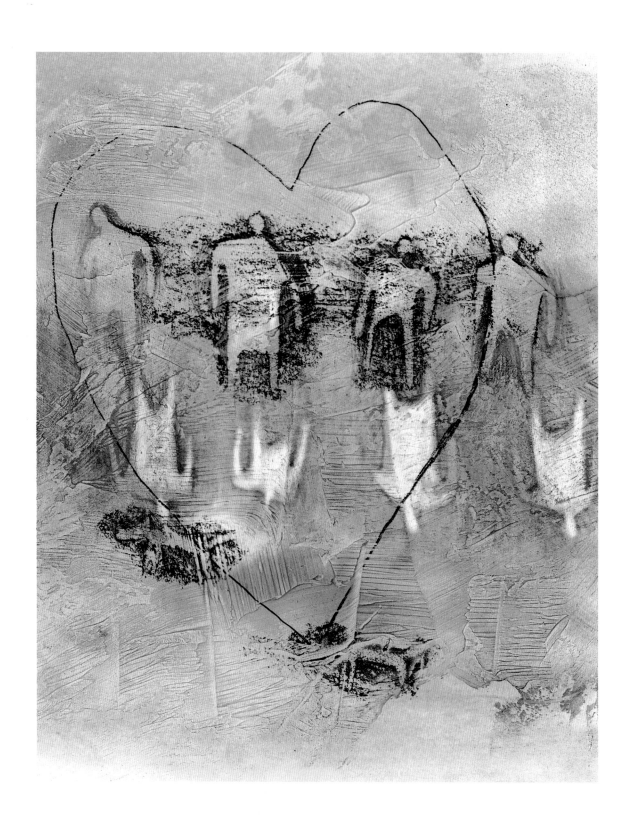

Red Wood Reservation South Dakota USA
March 12th 1859

Mr President,

I am writing on behalf of my people. We would like to know why the
white men do not like us. My tribe is peaceful. Our children use the skill
of the mighty bow and arrow for hunting, not for murder. My people
have been moved further and further west to make room for the white
men and we have not complained. Just because we carry arrows in
quivers and have bows on our backs we are considered to be terrorists.
My people love the freshness of the air around us, the wind blowing in
our faces as we gallop across the rolling prairies. The stars lead us on
through the dark, velvet night. They show us the way to a beautiful
valley, undiscovered. My people are safe here; they love the tranquility
and peacefulness of the stream meandering through the valley, the
chuckles and the gurgles that arise from the water goddess, as she
happily plays through the thicket, dancing to a mysterious melody.
Then the great iron monster stomped towards the valley. Out of one arm
poured a sticky, grey substance and a few minutes after it touched the
ground it hardened, and the luscious green grass beneath it was lost.
We fled till we found another valley, but this valley is an enclosure,
a reservation.

   We cannot go anywhere else for it is against white man's law to go into
white man's land. Our freedom, our peace is lost. There used to be a
hundred of us in my tribe but now there are only ten because you people
have been shooting us one by one. Our buffalo herds are now in the
happy hunting ground and our children's stomachs are empty. Your
people will not be happy until every green patch of grass is a hard, grey
layer of concrete.

   Not until every woodland is a town will you be happy and most of all
you want to see an Indian-free land. Why can't white men and our
Indian tribes live together in harmony? We have hearts too and we hope
that your fellow members of government have enough heart to grant us
our wish.

From an Indian with a peaceful heart,

Whistling Wind

Jenny Price, age 10 Oakleigh House School Swansea

Illustration by Malcolm Phipps

My dear children,

I am dying, and I want to take one last opportunity to tell you how much I love you and how much your actions have hurt me.

I gave life to your parents and their parents before them. I provided you with the food you needed, with fresh water and with clean air to breathe.

The rivers and seas are my life blood. You have clogged my arteries with your untreated sewage and with chemicals from your factories. This had killed so much of the sea life which was there for your benefit. You have been greedy. You over-fished and over-hunted, putting at risk your food supplies and endangering some of my most beautiful creatures - the whales.

I can no longer breathe because you have cut down so many of my life-giving trees. Without their vital oxygen we will all die, but you put profit before our very lives, and my tears have not turned to acid rain.

My face is marked and scarred by your bombs and guns and my body is the burial ground for the victims of your wars.

I have said goodbye to the many old friends who will soon be joined by others: the tiger, the elephant, the rhinoceros and the panda. Unless you act now to mend your ways, they will be joined by you and I.

Please help me!

Mother Earth

Heather Hughes, age 9 Lochfield Primary School Paisley

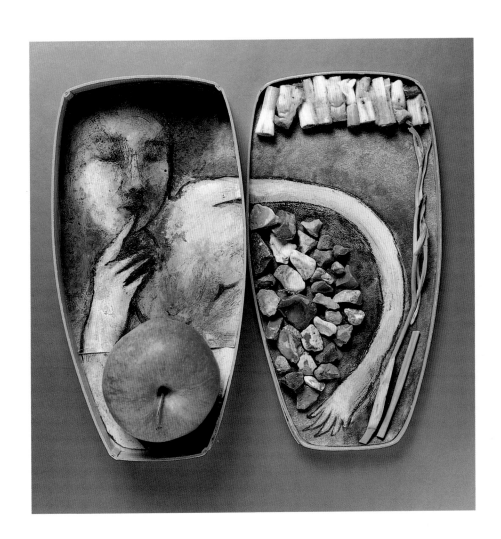

Dobrinja, Sarajevo 19th February 1994

Dear Anna,

I'm writing this to you at 6.30 in the morning and the city outside is in ruins which is being covered with a blanket of snow. This is the first time in months that I have woken up to the sound of silence: the snipers have stopped firing and the shells have stopped pounding in the streets above us.

This peace seems to be the miracle that we have all been waiting for in hope for almost two years, the moment when the sounds to be heard will be those of my children happily playing outside without any fear of danger.

These are my darling children who, after two years growing up in a battlefield no longer know what peace is and they cannot imagine a life without war. One of the games they play together

is 'The News'. It makes me cry to watch them tell each other that 'peace negotiations are being made', that 'food shortages are coming to an end' and that war will soon come to its end once the enemy troops have been pulled out of the country and that normal life will then resume. They imitate what they hear us talking about, not realizing what it means or how they will be affected by what is happening around them. Some days we cannot even go outside to buy a loaf of bread. Last week Franca next door was hit by a piece of shrapnel which sank into her leg as she went to collect a food parcel from the relief workers.

But now I feel as if suddenly we are free and can at last continue our lives as they were before all this terrible fighting began. Perhaps the storm has now cleared and we will soon catch a ray of sunshine peeping through the clouds. Perhaps my children will at last be able to learn what peace really is: to feel it, to smell it, to see it and to live with it.

Maybe one day you will be able to come back and live here with us again. We all miss you but are glad that you are both safe now. I have heard that the hospitals where you are are very good.

When Stefan comes home from work he says that the situation in the hospitals here is getting worse and worse. There are now only enough beds for half of the patients. The rest have to share or some of the very badly wounded ones are rescued by people from the Red Cross who take them out of the country to other hospitals.

We have been on the waiting list to be evacuated from here for a long time now, but maybe we will not need to go if this cease-fire holds.

I hope this letter reaches you, but it may not as couriers are difficult to find now, and the postal service is virtually non-existent. It would mean so much to us if we could have a letter from you, but I know that there is little chance of one ever reaching us. Communications have been make very difficult recently. There are road blockades everywhere and even relief workers are having trouble reaching us. (If this ever reaches you it will probably be through one of them). I hope you are all still well.

All my love,
Lucia

PS. It's now 7.54 and all my hopes of peace have just been shattered. The first gun shot of the day has just been fired and is now being answered by a barrage of gunfire. How many more people will be killed today, I wonder? I hope that this time it won't be my turn.

Lucia Ashmore, age 14
Redland High School for Girls Bristol

Illustrations by Ben Sedley

Dear Melissa,
I think it
is very
peaceful
when Logan
my dog
is not
barking.
Love from

Rebecca

Rebecca Yates, age 4 Lincolnshire

Illustration by Jo Stearn

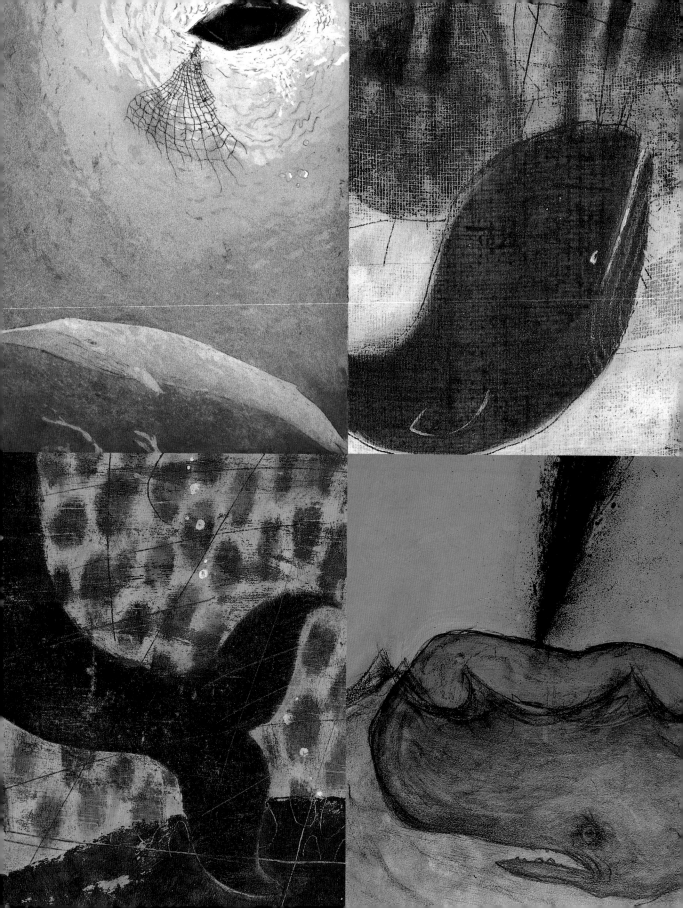

Dear Man,

I am a blue whale and I live in the Pacific Ocean. I am writing this letter to beg for peace in the oceans of the world on behalf of the creatures of the sea, who, like me, live beneath you in the Underworld. For years and years we have lived here, lived with the rhythmic rolling and swaying of currents rippling around us, gently sliding over our bodies and slipping past us silently to carry on towards their destiny. We have lived among the tall, silky corals that grow up from the sea bed, gracefully fluttering their fronds. We have swum among the gentle waves as they softly caress each rock that lies protecting thousands of small, defenceless creatures from their hungry enemies.

Yet you turn this tranquillity that we live in to a tormented, angry, fighting sea. The waves no longer sway peacefully but boil and swell in huge currents, rising up and hurling frothy, churned-up mouthfuls of spray into the air. As you dump piles of black, smelly oil into our clear water it becomes dark and murky with the filth. Oil wraps itself cruelly in a coat around so many beautiful sea birds and fish that once lived but now have perished as they were imprisoned by this deadly substance. It stuck to their feathers and clung to their eyes and mouths. It poisoned them and suffocated them. It killed them. You killed them.

You kill us whales too. You hunt us in big ships. You follow us. When you have us trapped between ships, you drop a net down. We are victims to you, just like the birds and fish are victims to oil. The picture of a net advancing, cutting through the water from all sides, fills us with alarm. The feeling of sheer panic that overcomes us as we see no way out, as the strong wires in the net press tightly against our bodies, is one you could never imagine.

Yet our worst nightmare is being harpooned. The deadly spear is directed towards our bodies. It implants itself firmly into us. The dire pain as it sears through our bodies makes us writhe about in agony. I cannot even begin to describe the feelings we have to endure. When the harpoon gun pierces us and sinks further into our flesh, barbs hold it there and prevent it from coming out. The result can be seen in the surrounding water which turns a deep, bloody red and is polluted with our death.

I have not experienced this myself, and luckily I am alive and able to write this letter to you. Many of my friends, however, and family, are now dead and it is as much for them as for anyone else that I am pleading to you to stop doing this. You are driving us to death, driving us to extinction. Please, give us peace.

Yours beseechingly,
Blue Whale

Louise Plater, age 13 Christleton High School Chester

Illustrations by Debra McFarlane, Sarah Markes & Sean Carney

To all the people fighting in Bosnia.

When I watch the news I feel the world is turning into a horrible place instead of a nice calm place. So I think I have a way to solve your problems. This is what we do at my school instead of fighting. We do talking out. This is how to do it. If someone does something horrible to you say please would you come with me and sit them down in a special quiet place. It could be sitting on a riverbank.

When we talk out we talk calmly and try to understand what the other person is feeling. This is a very hard thing to do but everyone in my school can do it. The secret is to throw away the thing you want to do and think about the other person. We talk and talk and talk until we agree on what to do. Why don't you try it?

Love from

Jamie Lindsay

Jamie Lindsay, age 7 Cavell First and Nursery School Norwich

Illustrations by Aude Van Ryn

Thank you

With special thanks from Newell and Sorrell, Royal Mail and Pavilion Books to all the young letter-writers, whose written work is reproduced in this book. Our thanks to course tutors Jake Abrams at Kingston University, Dan Fern at The Royal College of Art, Lawrence Zeegan at Camberwell College of Art, and Christopher Corr at Central Saint Martins.

And a big thank you to all the students who helped to illustrate this book, including those whose work didn't make it into the final selection. We couldn't have made this book without all of you.

The writers and the illustrators

Front cover
Illustration Sean Carney,
Lisa Wright & Kate Eadie
Kingston University

Endpaper
Illustration Sophie Thomas
Central St Martins

Page 4
Illustration Julie Monks
Kingston University

Page 7
Illustration Julie Monks
Kingston University

Page 8
Illustration Aude Van Ryn
Central St Martins

Page 10
Illustration John McFaul
Kingston University

Page 12
Letter Nicholas Harbottle
Illustration Sean Carney
Kingston University

Page 14
Letter Neil Bustin
Illustration Sarah Markes
Central St Martins

Page 16
Letter James Hilland
Illustration Charlie Kinsman
Central St Martins

Page 17
Letter Jonathan Glassington
Illustration Kate Tilley
Central St Martins

Page 18
Letter Geoffrey Lancaster
Illustration Peter Allsop
Kingston University

Page 20
Letter Joe McAuley
Illustration Claire McKenna
Central St Martins

Page 22
Letter Samantha Williams
Illustration Gill Button
Kingston University

Page 24
Letter David Lowe
Illustration Amanda Vigor
Royal College of Art

Page 26
Letter Rachel O'Neill
Illustration Susie Wilkinson
Camberwell College of Art

Page 27
Letter Louise Wakenshaw
Illustration Lucy Dawkins
Camberwell College of Art

Page 28
Letter Manvir Grewal
Illustration Marian Hill
Kingston University

Page 30
Letter David Lee Monaghio
Illustration Mark Ashcroft
Kingston University

Page 31
Letter Jacqui Dearden
Illustration Sophie Thomas
Central St Martins

Page 32
Letter Grainne O'Reilly
Illustration Michelle Thompson
Royal College of Art

Page 34
Letter Claire Turnbull
Illustration Vanessa Dell
Kingston University

Page 36
Letter Martina Gallogly
Illustration Ed Taylor
Kingston University

Page 37
Letter Julia Moffat
Illustration Kes James
Kingston University

Page 38
Letter Rebecca Marriott
Illustration Sophie Thomas
Central St Martins

Page 40
Letter Graham Sykes
Illustration Leonie Lord
Central St Martins

Page 41
Letter Siobhan Sippy
Illustration Alyson Waller
Kingston University

Page 42
Letter Philip Straughan
Illustration Gill Button
& Adam Ealovega
Kingston University

Page 44
Letter Scott Elliott
Illustration Amy Smith
Central St Martins

Page 46
Letter Jane Moffat
Illustration Julie Baker
Kingston University

Page 48
Letter Charles Siem
Illustration Elizabeth le Court
Kingston University

Page 49
Letter James Woolrich
Illustration Sarah Markes
Central St Martins

Page 50
Letter Adele Rebecca Hardy
Illustration Tiphanie Beeke
Royal College of Art

Illustration by Annabel Hill